CW00815989

THE
Dirty Girl's
JOKE BOOK
2

THIS IS A CARLTON BOOK

Text, illustrations, design copyright © 2005
Carlton Books Limited

This edition published by
Carlton Books Limited 2005
20 Mortimer Street
London W1T 3JW

A CIP catalogue record for this book is
available from the British Library
ISBN 1 84442 570 3

executive editor: **Lisa Dyer**

art editor: **Zoë Dissell**

editor: **Lara Maiklem**

design: **Penny Stock**

production controller: **Caroline Alberti**

illustrator: **Anna Hymas**

Printed and bound in Great Britain

THE
Dirty Girl's
JOKE BOOK
2

CARLTON
BOOKS

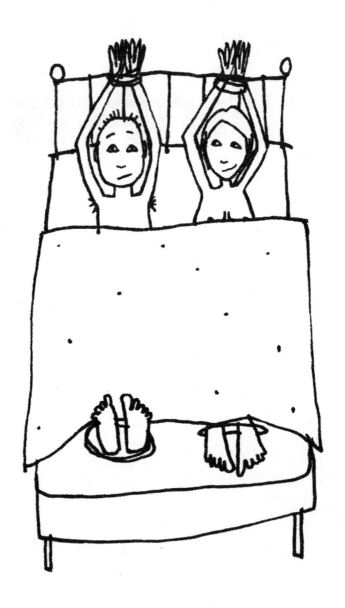

CONTENTS

FIRST
IMPRESSIONS

Fancy a quickie?
Can you do any other kind?

I'm an expert in mouth-to-mouth resuscitation – want a demonstration?
I'd have to be completely dead before I let you get that close.

I can give you supersex.
I'll take the soup, thanks.

Do you like it doggy style?
Yes – you can beg all you like, and
I'll roll over and play dead.

What's your sign?

'Private Property.'

Can I give you my number?

Yes, I'll call you when my dog's on heat.

I'd like to get into your pants.

I already have one arsehole
in my pants, thanks.

Hey, angel, pull up a cloud and sit down.
Sorry, angels can only talk to people who are dead
– dead from the neck up doesn't qualify.

Your place or mine?

Well... I'm running out of places to hide the bodies at mine...

I've got a telepathic watch. It tells me you're not wearing any underwear.
I'm afraid I am wearing underwear.
Damn the thing's an hour fast again.

**What's a nice girl like you doing
in a place like this?**

If I were a nice girl, I wouldn't be in a place like this.

That dress is very
becoming on you.
**But the question is –
would I be coming
on you?**

**Are you an optical spanner? Because
every time you look at me I feel my
nuts tighten.**

Lucky you've got nuts because you're not
getting a screw.

Nice legs – what time
do they open?
**Sorry, it's full
members only.**

If I bought you some underwear, would there be anything in it for me? **Yes, the knowledge that you'd made my boyfriend very happy.**

If we are what we eat, I could be you by tomorrow morning.
No, by tomorrow morning you'll be 18 pints of lager and a kebab.

Do you come here often?
No, it's just the way I laugh.

Would you like another drink?
No, if one doesn't make you look attractive, I don't think two will do the trick.

I'm a magician – want to see my wand?
Can it make you disappear?

A 13-year-old boy goes into a pub and says to the barmaid, 'Get me a double Scotch on the rocks.' **'What do you want to do,'** asks the barmaid, **'get me in trouble?'** 'Maybe later,' says the kid, 'but I'll start with the Scotch.'

Where have you been all my life? **Where I'll be the rest of your life – in your wildest dreams.**

I like an intelligent woman.
Yes – they say that opposites attract.

I could make you the happiest woman on earth.
You're leaving so soon?

Haven't I seen you somewhere before?

Yes, that's why I stopped going there.

I wish you were a door – I could bang you all day.

I doubt it; you haven't got a key that would fit my lock.

You've got lovely eyes...

Yes, they saw you coming.

Why is a beautiful girl like you still single?

Just lucky, I guess.

We could be having wild sex by midnight tonight.

We probably will be – but not with each other.

Where have you been all my life?
Outside your window, in the bushes, with the binoculars.

**Is that a ladder in your stocking
or a stairway to heaven?**

You have to be good to go to heaven. Really good.

Can I buy you a drink?

Can I just have the money?

HOW DO
YOU
KNOW
WHEN?

How do you know when you're in bed with a policeman?

He asks you to blow into his breathalyzer.

How do you know when you're in bed with a fireman?

He comes when you're hot and leaves you soaking wet.

How do you know when you're in bed with a mathematician?

He divides your legs and then he subtracts his root so you don't multiply.

How do you know when you're in bed with a postman?

He doesn't come when he's supposed to, and half the time it's in the wrong box.

How do you know when you're in bed with an explorer?

He goes deeper into the bush than any man has ever been.

How do you know when you're in bed with an astronaut?

The equipment is huge, but there's no atmosphere.

How do you know when you're in bed with a takeaway chef? **You ask for 69 and he gives you egg-fried rice.**

How do you know when you're in bed with an archaeologist?

They'll date anything.

How do you know when you're in bed with a blacksmith?

He hammers away for hours and then he makes a bolt for the door.

How do you know when you've found Mr Right?

His first name is 'Always'.

How can you tell when your husband is dead?

The sex is the same, but the smell of farts has vanished.

How do you know when a man's been taking iron tablets and Viagra?

Every time he gets excited he points North.

How can you tell when a woman is frigid?

When she opens her legs a light comes on.

Why did God create alcohol?
So ugly people could get laid.

How can you tell when a man
is well-hung?

**His face is blue and he's
stopped struggling.**

**How do you know when
you're getting old?**
You can sleep with someone half
your age without breaking any laws.

How do you know when you're
using food as a substitute for sex?

**You can't even get into your
own pants.**

**How do you know when a man
is sexually aroused?**
He has a pulse.

How do you know when a truckload of Viagra has fallen in the river Thames?

Tower Bridge stays open for hours.

How do you know when a hitch-hiker is a witch?

When she strokes the driver's leg he turns into a lay-by.

How do you get a man to always leave the toilet seat down?

Cut off his penis.

What is 69 + 69?

Dinner for four.

Why do men get married?

So they can stop holding their stomachs in.

Why are men's brains bigger than women's brains?
So they can think of excuses.

How do you spot the sex-crazed whale?
She's the one who'll suck the end off a submarine and swallow the seamen.

Why do they name hurricanes after women?
Because they're wild and wet and noisy when they come – and when they go you lose your house and your car.

Why are breasts like toy trains?
They're both intended for children but usually get played with by men.

What food diminishes your sex drive by 75%?

Wedding cake.

Why does only one sperm out of millions get to the egg?

Because they refuse to stop and ask for directions.

Why does a penis have a big head on the end?

To stop the man's hand sliding off and hitting him in the eye.

Why is Viagra like an amusement park?

They both make you wait two hours for a three-minute ride.

Why is sex like playing bridge?

If you don't have a good partner you'd better have a good hand.

Why do female spiders bite the heads off their mates after sex?

It's the only way to stop them snoring.

Why is a dildo like a soya bean?

They're both a poor substitute for meat.

Why are men like tights?

They never quite fit between the legs, and
they usually run after one night out.

Why can't Miss Piggy count to 70?

Because when she gets to 69 she has a frog
in her throat.

Why do women prefer a circumcised penis?

Because anything with 10% off is always attractive.

When did Pinocchio realize he was made of wood?

When his hand caught fire.

If mothers have Mother's Day and fathers have Father's Day, what do bachelors have?

Palm Sunday.

What's a shotgun wedding?

It's a wife-or-death situation.

Why doesn't Popeye's favourite tool go rusty?

He puts it in Olive Oil.

How do you know which girl in a convent school is head girl?

She's the one with the dirty knees.

How do you get a man to really listen to what you say?

Talk in your sleep.

Why is a one-night stand like a newsflash?

It's unexpected, brief and probably a disaster.

Why do men feel more confident with computers than women?

No computer ever laughed at a three-and-a-half-inch floppy.

Why do women get PMT and cellulite?

God made Man first, and he just couldn't help making a few helpful suggestions.

Why are men like clothes shops?

They're most interesting when their clothes are 50% off.

Why do men close their eyes during sex?

They can't stand to see a woman enjoying herself.

COMEBACKS
AND
PUTDOWNS

If my dog looked like you,
I'd shave its bum and train
it to walk backwards.

Is your name Ex-Lax?
Because you're irritating
the shit out of me.

Save your breath – you'll need it to blow up your girlfriend.

I heard you're nobody's fool. Never mind, maybe someone will adopt you.

Do you always use contraception?
Yes...
Good, so you learned from your
parents' mistake.

If you took an IQ test the results would come back negative.

I didn't know they did condoms in cheese-and-onion flavour! Oh, sorry, you haven't put one on yet…

What's the best position to make an ugly baby?
I don't know.
Well, call your mum, because she certainly does.

Will you miss me?
Why don't you go away and we'll find out.

Sorry, I'm not your type – I'm not inflatable.

A rich man loses his job and tells the wife they'll have to economize. 'If you could learn to cook and clean and do the laundry,' he says, 'we could sack the housekeeper.'
'And if you could learn to do cunnilingus,' she replies, 'we could sack the chauffeur.'

I bet you're not a virgin.
You're right – because not all men are as ugly as you.

Go out? Yes, we could go to the zoo. They must be wondering where you've been.

Just because you have a prick, doesn't mean you have to act like one.

I bet when you call one of those telephone sex lines, the woman on the other end gets an earache.

Have you thought of blind dating? Then you'd only frighten them off with the smell.

You should tell your trousers that it's rude to point.

Don't let your mind wander – it's too small to be out on its own.

Is that your birthday suit? You should have asked, I could have ironed it for you.

Go out with you? Sorry, I was about to call Greenpeace and tell them to come and float you off the beach.

Why not chat up someone your own size – like the QE2?
Where did you meet your last girlfriend? Battersea Dogs' Home?

You'd better get in training – I hear that 'ugly' is going to be an Olympic sport.

My dog wouldn't fuck you – not even if you had a pork chop tied round your neck.

You must be a man of rare intelligence – either rare or completely extinct.

Did you know light travels faster than sound? That's why you seemed quite bright till you opened your mouth.

I'd love to fuck your brains out, but it looks like someone else got there first.

If I throw a stick, will you leave?

If I blindfold my dog, I might get it to hump your leg.

You know, you have the body of a god – Buddha.

Tell me everything you know —
I have 20 seconds to spare.

I'd like to leave you with one thought... It'd be one more than you've had all evening.

You know, you make me think about sperm.
Why?
Because you too have a one-in-three million chance, with the help of a woman, of ever becoming a human being.

WHAT'S
THE
DIFFERENCE
BETWEEN...?

What's the difference between sex and water-skiing?

Nothing. They both start with getting wet between the legs and end up with you on your back.

What's the difference between a man and a cup of coffee?

A cup of coffee can keep you awake all night.

What's the difference between parsley and pubic hair?

A man will push the parsley aside and keep eating.

What's the difference between parsley and pussy?

Nobody eats parsley.

What's the difference between a man and a Rubik cube?

No matter how long you play with a Rubik cube, it'll still be hard.

What's the difference between a penis and chocolate?

Chocolate's still satisfying after it's gone soft in your hand.

What's the difference between a clitoris and a golf ball?

Men will spend hours looking for a golf ball.

What's the difference between a man and a battery?

A battery has a positive side.

What's the difference between a sin and a shame?

It's a sin to put it in, but it's a shame to take it out.

What's the difference between a man and a lava lamp?

You only have to turn a lava lamp on once, and it will go up and down indefinitely.

What's the difference between
a beer and a man?

**The beer comes in a can,
not in your mouth.**

**What's the difference between
a dove and a swallow?**

One's the bird of peace and
the other's the bird of true love.

What's the difference between
a condom and a coffin?

**A stiff comes in one and
goes out in the other.**

**What's the difference between
a turkey and a penis?**

It's worth waking up at five in the morning
to put a turkey in, because it always lasts
long enough to satisfy everyone.

What's the difference between a blood test nurse and a prostitute?

One gets paid to prick lots of fingers and the other gets paid to finger lots of pricks.

What's the difference between a slag and a bitch?

A slag sleeps with everyone. A bitch sleeps with everyone except you.

What's the difference between a bankrupt and a man who takes Viagra?

They're both hard up, but the bankrupt can't spend any more.

What's the difference between a man and a Slinky?

Nothing. They're both slightly amusing when they're falling down the stairs, but are otherwise useless.

What's the difference between a lesbian carpenter and a straight carpenter?

One uses tongue and groove, and the other just screws.

What's the difference between medium and rare?

Five inches is medium, ten inches is rare.

What's the difference between a man and a holiday?

Nothing – neither of them is ever long enough.

What's the difference between an infant and an adult?

Infancy isn't nearly as much fun as adultery.

What's the difference between a man and a nappy?

You can change a nappy.

What's the difference between a blonde and a lawyer?

There are some things even a blonde won't do.

What's the difference between monogamy and monotony?

Er – nothing.

What's the difference between a circus and a singles bar?

At a circus the clowns don't talk.

What's the difference between a clitoris and a remote control?

A man can put his hand straight on the remote control without looking – every time.

What's the difference between a sweater and a jumper?

With a sweater your sheets are always soaking – with a jumper you don't dare bend over to put them in the washing machine.

What's the difference between a man and a ten-pence coin?

Every time you toss the coin, you have a 50/50 chance of getting head.

What's the difference between a penis and a redundancy cheque?

It's always fun to blow a man's redundancy cheque.

What's the difference between a cockpit and a box office?

A box office is a place that tries to ensure everyone has a satisfying evening's entertainment. A cockpit is really only concerned with getting up and down.

What's the difference between a gay prince and a book-lover?

A book-lover uses a bookmark – a gay prince likes his pages bent over.

What's the difference between a man a lawnmower?

You don't have to suck a lawnmower's exhaust pipe to get it to cut the grass.

What's the difference between a trombonist and a man who plays alto and tenor saxophones?

One's horny and one's bisaxual.

What's the difference between an unlucky mouse and a lucky cock?

Nothing – they both end up inside a satisfied pussy.

What's the difference between circumcision and divorce?

Divorce gets rid of the whole prick.

What's the difference between cinema snacks and pictures of naked policemen?

One's popcorn and the other's cop porn!

What's the difference between a child car seat and a condom?

One stops kids in the back seat causing accidents, the other stops accidents in the back seat causing kids.

What's the difference between a curtain
and an erection?

**A curtain doesn't come down until the
performance is finished.**

**What's the difference between
men and concrete?**

Both take ages to get hard, but concrete
only has to be laid once.

When a man talks dirty to a woman
it's sexual harassment.

**When a woman talks dirty to a man it's
£1.60 a minute.**

According to a recent survey, men say the first thing
that they notice about women are their eyes. Women
say the first thing they notice about men is that they're
a bunch of liars.

**Most popular female fantasy?
Having sex with your boyfriend's
best friend, a film star, or a stranger
on a train.**

Most popular male fantasy?
Having sex with a woman who isn't fantasizing
about somebody else.

What's the difference between a man and a computer?

1. A computer can do more than one job at once.

2. A computer will remember what you told it yesterday.

3. A computer is more impressive the smaller it is.

4. If your computer doesn't have enough hard drive, you can upgrade it.

5. You can still get your work done after you turn a computer on.

6. With a computer, faster is always better.

7. A computer knows the difference between your inbox and your outbox.

8. A computer is more likely to go down on you.

9. A computer can communicate with other computers using words as well as sounds and pictures.

10. A computer can remember important dates like birthdays.

What's the difference between a man and a Christmas tree?

1. The Christmas tree goes up and comes down when you decide it's time.

2. A Christmas tree's balls are nice to look at.

3. No-one thinks any worse of you for having an artificial Christmas tree instead of a live one.

4. A Christmas tree doesn't mind when you add an electric device to improve the effect.

5. You can ignore a Christmas tree for 11 months and it'll still be ready next time you want it.

What's the difference between a man and a cat?

1. The only thing a cat leaves all over the house is hair.

2. When a cat sticks its bum in your face, it's not expecting you to lick it.

3. A cat won't fake affection to get what it wants.

4. Cats don't want to watch the football.

5. You can stroke a cat twice without it trying to put its tail in your mouth.

6. A cat won't bring you flowers after it's been out all night screwing the neighbour's cat.

7. A hairy back looks good on a cat.

8. Cats can wash themselves.

9. A man only wishes he could lick his own genitals.

10. BUT, if a man brings you a present of a dead animal, it's already been made into a coat.

What's the difference between a man and a motorbike?

1. You can tell how big the exhaust pipe is before you start riding it.

2. You can swap motorbikes with your friend to see which is the better ride.

3. It's the motorbike that suffers if you don't use enough lubrication.

4. A motorbike stays between your legs till you've had enough fun.

5. You only chain a motorbike up when you've finished riding it.

MORE **SHAGGY** BITCH STORIES

'I don't know what to get my wife for her birthday,' **says Bob, 'She already has everything, and she earns more than I do, so she can afford to buy anything she wants.' 'Why don't you give her a voucher saying she can have 60 minutes of great sex, any way she wants?' asks his friend. 'Well, I can't think of anything else,' says Bob, 'So I'll give it a try**The next day, Bob's back in the bar. 'I gave her the voucher,' he says. 'Did she like it?' asks his friend. 'Oh yes! She loved it. She kissed me, thanked me for the best present I'd ever given her, and then she ran out of the door shouting,** "I'll be back in an hour!"'

When John Wayne Bobbit's wife cut off his penis, she drove away with it and threw it out of the car window. Before it landed in the field, it hit the windscreen of another car and bounced off. In the car, a little girl was being driven home by her mother. **'Wow!'** said the girl, **'What was THAT?'** 'Nothing, honey,' replied her embarrassed mother, 'just a fly.' **'Well,'** says the girl, **'for a little fly, it had a huge willy.'**

A man goes away on a business trip and, as it's a very swanky hotel, his wife comes to join him for the weekend. They have a nice dinner in the restaurant, a drink in the bar, and then they can't wait to go up to their room. In fact, they can't even wait that long – as soon as they get into the lift they're all over each other. The man is pulling her panties down and in less than a minute they're at it. Unfortunately, the doors open at the next floor and the chambermaid gets in. 'Well, really!' says the chambermaid. 'I'm sorry,' says the woman, 'we just had a couple of drinks and got a bit carried away. I don't normally behave this way.' 'I'm sure you don't,' says the chambermaid, 'but this is the fourth time this week I've caught him at it.'

A young priest was taking confession in a convent school for the first time. **'Bless me, Father, for I have sinned,'** says the first schoolgirl, **'I had impure thoughts about my teacher.'** 'Impure thoughts – that's four Hail Marys,' says the priest. **'Bless me, Father,'** says the second schoolgirl, **'I stole a pencil from the stationary cupboard.'** 'Stealing – that's six Hail Marys,' says the priest. But the third schoolgirl says, **'Bless me, Father, for I have sinned. I gave my boyfriend a blowjob behind the bike sheds.'** The priest is flummoxed – he's never heard this before, and he doesn't know what penance to impose. Slipping out of the confessional, he meets one of the nuns in the chapel. 'Quick, Sister Lillian,' he whispers, 'What does the Father Colin usually give for a blowjob?' 'Twenty quid,' she replies.

Cinderella's going to the ball. 'Dress – yes. Crystal carriage – yes. Handsome coachmen – yes. There's just one more thing I need, Fairy Godmother.' 'What's that, my dear?' 'I don't have any contraception.' The Fairy Godmother looks around and sees a pumpkin. With a wave of her wand, she turns it into a diaphragm. 'Off you go, Cinderella, but remember – you must be home by midnight or your dress will turn back into rags, your carriage will revert to a coal scuttle, the coachmen will be mice again and – most important – your diaphragm will turn back into a pumpkin!' **Cinderella promises to be back by midnight, pops the diaphragm in, and goes off to the ball. At five o'clock in the morning, Cinderella finally rolls in, dressed in rags,**

carrying
a coal
scuttle full
of mice, but
smiling happily.
'Where have you
been?' asks Fairy
Godmother, 'I told you to
be back by midnight!' 'I know,' sighs
Cinderella, 'but I met such a nice man.'
'Prince Charming?' 'No, his name was
Peter Peter something...'

A man rings his brother, but the brother's wife answers the phone. 'Can I speak to George?' 'No, I'm afraid George is dead.' 'What? When did that happen?' 'Last night – he died in bed.' 'How terrible. Did he have any last requests?' 'Yes, his last words were "Please, put down the gun."'

Little Red Riding Hood is walking through the forest with her basket when out hops a little rabbit. **'Oh, be careful, Little Red Riding Hood,'** says the rabbit, **'The Big Bad Wolf is out hunting. If he catches you, he'll pull up your skirt, pull down your panties and shag you!'** 'Thanks for the warning,' replies Little Red Riding Hood, 'but I'll be okay.' A little further along the path a squirrel pops out of a tree. **'Oh, be careful, Little Red Riding Hood,'** says the squirrel, **'The Big Bad Wolf is out hunting. If he catches you, he'll pull up your skirt, pull down your panties and shag you!'**

' replies Little Red Riding
e okay.' After half a mile, the
t of the bushes and confronts
'Now I've caught you,'
ing to pull up your
ur panties and shag

Little Red Riding Hood
sket and pulls out a gun.
nting her gun right at the
re going to **eat me**, just

A woman is lying in bed with her lover when she hears her husband coming in. 'Quick!,' **she says to her lover,** 'There's no time to get dressed. Stand in the corner and I'll cover you with talcum powder.' **In comes the husband and he immediately asks, 'Is that a new statue?' 'That's right,' replies the wife, 'The Smiths had one in their bedroom and I liked it so much I got one, too.' The husband says nothing else, but gets into bed, leaving the 'statue' standing as still as he can in the corner. Around four in the morning, the husband gets up and comes back with a cup of tea and a plate of biscuits, which he puts down beside the 'statue'.** 'There,' **he says,** 'have a biscuit. I was stuck in the Smiths' bedroom for three days, and nobody offered me so much as a drink of water.'

An old lady phones the fire brigade in the middle of the night. 'Please come at once – a couple of big hairy bikers are outside, trying to climb up to my bedroom window.' **'Madam, we're the fire brigade – you need to call the police.'** 'Why? I thought you were the ones with the ladders!'

A convict escapes from gaol, breaks into a house and ties up the young couple that are naked in bed.

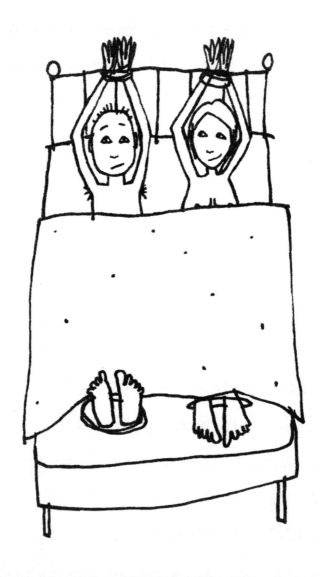

As they lie there, helpless, the wife says, 'Look, we'll do anything you ask. Take what you want – money, food, the car, anything, but don't hurt us.' The convict replies, 'Well, I've been in gaol for 20 years now. I've had nothing to eat but bread and water, I've had nothing to do but sew mailbags and I haven't set eyes on a woman in all that time.' **Before the wife can say anything, the husband says, 'Take whatever you want. Don't kill us and we'll do anything you want. Anything.' 'Well then, roll over pretty boy. You remind me of my last cellmate.'**

A businessman goes to Japan to meet an important client. On his first evening there he meets a beautiful Japanese girl and, in spite of the language barrier, they end up in his hotel room. All night long they have the most amazing sex and every time he feels that he can't go on any more, she starts shouting, **'Hitakushi! Hitakushi!'** He's not sure what it means, but from the way she's shouting he's guessing that she's having a good time, so he feels like a bit of a stud. The next day, tired but pleased with himself, he meets the client on the golf course, and they talk business over a round of golf. The deal is almost clinched when they reach the 18th hole and the client hits a hole in one. **'Hitakushi!'** shouts the businessman. The client looks very cross and shouts back at the businessman,

'What do you mean, wrong hole?'

A man turns 40 and decides to treat himself to a facial. Sure enough, he **walks out looking much younger, and feeling very pleased with himself.** As he stands in the queue at the Post Office he asks the guy at the counter how old he thinks he is. '30 maybe?' 'No! I'm actually 40 today!' **And he walks out, very pleased with himself. He goes into the paper shop and asks the newsagent how old he thinks he is. 'I don't know – 29? 28?' 'No! I'm actually 40 today!' He's feeling really good now, and when he gets to the bus stop he asks an old lady sitting on the bench how old she thinks he is.** 'To tell you the truth,' she replies, 'my eyesight isn't what it was, but years ago I worked in a laboratory and we devised a sure-fire scientific method of telling a man's age.' **'Really?' asks the man, thinking if he can fool a scientific method, he must be looking hot-to-trot.** 'Yes,' replies the old lady, 'shall I try it

on you?' So the man agrees and quick as a flash the old lady puts her hand down his trousers, inside his pants, and starts feeling his cock with an expression of intense concentration. After five minutes she pulls her hand out and says, 'You are 40 years old – in fact, today is your birthday.' 'Amazing!' replies the man, 'You're right! How did you know that?' 'I was behind you in the queue at the Post Office.'

A couple go skiing, and the man loses his gloves. When they get back to the chalet, he says his hands are frozen. **'Well,' says the woman, 'put them between my thighs and warm them up.'** The second day, the same thing happens – he can't find his gloves, his hands are frozen, and he puts them between her thighs to warm them up. On the third day he gets up and asks, **'Honey, have you seen my ear-warmers?'**

An old lighthouse keeper lives alone with his wife on a remote rock, until a young assistant is sent to join them. On the first day, the young assistant offers to take the first watch at the top of the lighthouse, so the keeper and his wife can have some time together. 'But no shagging,' he says. 'I'm here without a wife or girlfriend, so it wouldn't be fair.' The keeper and his wife stroll along the beach hand-in-hand, and the assistant shouts down, 'Hey! No shagging!' 'We're not shagging,' calls the keeper, 'we're just holding hands.' They go and sit outside the keeper's cottage and do a crossword together, but the assistant shouts down, 'Hey! I said no shagging! It's not fair!' 'We're not shagging!' answers the keeper. After lunch, the wife offers to show the assistant around the island, and the keeper goes to the top of the lighthouse. 'Well, I never!' he says to himself. 'From up here, it does look exactly like they're shagging!'

Aguy sits in a bar wearing jeans, a checked shirt, cowboy boots, and a Stetson hat. A woman comes in, also wearing a checked shirt, jeans, cowboy boots, and a hat and asks, **'Say, are you a real cowboy?'** 'Well,' he answers, 'my whole life has been spent working with cattle – rounding up cows, roping calves, branding steers, and wrestling bulls. Yep, I reckon I must be a real cowboy. But what about you – can I buy you a drink, cowgirl?' **'No thanks, cowboy,'** replies the woman, **'you see, I'm a lesbian.'** 'What's that?' **'Well, I love women. I wake up in the morning and think about women; I get in the shower and imagine a naked woman there with me; I think about**

women all day long and the last thing on my mind before I go to sleep is women.'

'Fair enough,' says the cowboy. A few minutes later, another woman comes in and asks him the same question,

'Are you a real cowboy?'

'Well,' he says, 'all my life I thought I was a real cowboy, but I just found out I'm a lesbian.'

A couple move into a flat with very thin walls, and they're worried that the neighbours will hear them talking in bed. 'I know,' says the wife, 'when you want sex, put your hand on my breast and squeeze once. If you don't want sex, squeeze it twice.' **'Okay,' says the husband. 'If you want sex, put your hand on my penis and pull it once. If you don't want sex, pull it 50 times.'**

A woman fell off her balcony on the 23rd floor, and as she fell, she prayed, 'Oh God, please give me a chance to live!' Suddenly a man leant out from his balcony and caught her in his arms. Before she had a chance to thank him, he asked her, 'Do you suck?' 'Of course not!' she shouted, thinking this can't be what God intended. So the man let go and she fell again, hurtling towards the ground. Suddenly a second man put out his arms and caught her. 'Do you screw?' he asked. 'No!' she shouted, wondering what the hell God was playing at, sending all these perverts to catch her. So the man dropped her and she continued to fall. Just as death seemed certain, a third man put out his arms and caught her. Before he could say a word, the woman shouted, 'I suck! I screw!' 'Slut!' cried the man, and dropped her to her death.

SIZE
MATTERS

Why do men give their willies names?

Because it's always good to be on first-name terms with the boss.

Mr Smith hires a gardener who says he's got a huge penis – a foot long relaxed, over a yard erect. When Mrs Smith hears this she wants to see, so she tells her husband to get the gardener to show it to him while she hides in the shed. **The next day, while Mr Smith and the gardener are cutting the hedge, Mr Smith asks to see the huge penis.** They go to the shed, where Mrs Smith is hiding, and the gardener gets it out. Impressed, Mr Smith asks to see it erect, so the gardener rubs it till it grows to be a yard long. **The gardener then asks to see Mr Smith's penis, so he gets his out – it's pretty small. Even when he rubs it, it's only a few inches long.** That night, he says to his wife, 'I hope you're satisfied. I was pretty embarrassed when he asked to see mine, too. It looked so small next to that monster.' **'You were embarrassed? I couldn't think of what to say to all my friends from work that were in the shed with me?'**

A man loses his penis in an accident and the doctor offers him an experimental treatment – they'll take the trunk off a baby elephant and replace his penis with that. The operation goes well and he's told not to have sex for six weeks, until it's completely healed. The six weeks is over at last and the man is feeling very horny so he plans a romantic night out with his girlfriend at a nice restaurant. When they get there he feels even hornier and his penis starts to swell up. **Eventually, he has to unzip his fly and put a napkin over his lap to ease the pressure. The waiter puts a basket of bread on the table and immediately the penis**

pops out, grabs a bread roll and disappears with it under the napkin. The girlfriend is really impressed. 'Perhaps we should skip dessert,' she whispers. 'Can you do that again?' 'Probably,' says her boyfriend, 'but I don't think I can fit another bread roll up my arse.'

Who's the most popular guy in the singles bar?

The one in the corner, licking his eyebrows.

What three words do men hate to hear during sex?

Is it in?

What three words do women hate to hear during sex?

Honey, I'm home!

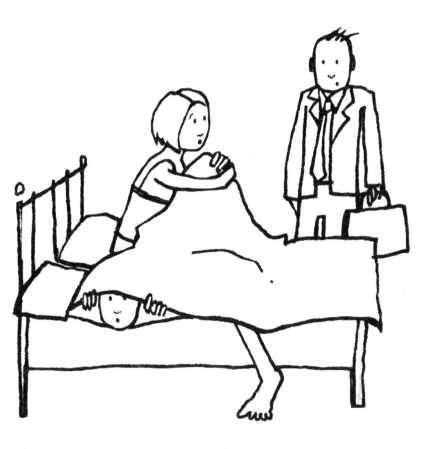

A man goes to a hypnotherapist to get help for his impotence. While he's hypnotized, the therapist tells him that next time he hears the words '1-2-3' he'll get a huge hard on. When he hears the words '1-2-3-4' it will go down again. The man wakes up and the therapist explains that all he needs to do is say the numbers to control his erection. Very excited, the man can't wait to get into bed with his wife. She's preparing to go straight to sleep as usual when he slips between the sheets and murmurs, '1-2-3'. Immediately, he starts to swell and gets a huge erection. Just as he's about to get amorous, his wife rolls over and asks, 'What did you say 1-2-3 for?'

One swallow doesn't make a summer – but it can make a man's day.

Men are just like children. You give them a lovely toy for their birthday but they're only happy if you let them play with the box it comes in.

How do you make your cock look bigger?

Buy smaller hens.

'I wanted sex with a fitter, more attractive man, so I signed my husband up for a slimming group.'

'Is it working?'

'Oh yes – he goes to the meetings every week – and while he's there his younger, fitter, more attractive brother comes round to my place.'

'Heard about the new Olympic condoms? They come in gold, gold and bronze.'

'Why no silver?'

'Do you think a man ever wants to come second?'

Why is sex like snow?

You never know how many inches you're going to get or how long before it turns to slush.

A woman walks into a chemist and asks if they sell extra-large condoms.

'Yes, we do – how many do you want?'

'I don't want to buy any – but if anybody else does, can you give them my phone number?'

Little Johnny is at the zoo with his parents, and he sees the male donkey getting rather excited. 'What's that, Dad?' he asks, pointing to the large thing he can see underneath the donkey. 'Ask your mother, son.' So little Johnny trots over to his mother. 'What's that, Mum?' 'That? That's nothing.' Little Johnny still isn't satisfied so he goes back to his dad. 'Dad, Dad – what is that? Mum said it was nothing.' 'Well, she's been spoilt.'

'Doctor, I don't seem to be able to get an erection.'

'I can't find anything seriously wrong – I think it's the effects of drinking.'

'I'll come back when you're sober then.'

A man goes to his doctor and says, 'D-d-d-d-doctor, y-you've g-g-got to h-h-h-help me! I c-c-c-can't l-live with this st-st-st-stutter any l-l-l-longer!' So the doctor examines him and says, 'This is a most unusual case. This stutter is caused by your penis.' 'M-m-m-my p-p-p-penis?' 'Yes, your penis is so long that it's putting strain on the vagus nerve, which is affecting your vocal cords. The only thing I can do is to remove half your penis.' Well, the man thinks hard, but eventually he says, 'A-a-all r-r-r-right d-d-d-doctor. I c-c-c-can't st-st-stand the sst-st-stuttering. D-d-d-do it!'

A month later, the same man comes back to see the doctor and says, 'Look, doctor, you've cured my stutter all right, but my wife says sex just isn't the same with a normal-sized penis. On balance, I think I'd rather put up with the stutter. Is there any way the operation can be reversed?' And the doctor replies, 'Nn-n-no, I'm afraid th-th-th-that's n-n-not p-p-p-possible.'

Why do men like big breasts and tight pussies?

Because they've got big mouths and small pricks.

At the fairground, a man sees a sign outside a tent: 'Make the horse laugh and win £100'. So he goes in. After two minutes the sound of horse laughter comes from the tent, and the man comes out and collects his £100. Next year, the fair is back, but this time the sign outside the tent reads 'Make the horse cry and win £100'. The same man goes in again, and after two minutes horsey sobs are coming from the tent. As the £100 is being counted out, the horse's owner asks the man what his secret is. 'Well, last year, I told that horse that my dick was bigger than his. That's why he laughed.' 'And this year?' 'This year, I didn't just tell him, I showed him.'

What do you get when you cross a chicken with an onion?

A cock that will bring tears to your eyes.

'My boyfriend can dial my telephone number with his tongue.'

'That's nothing, mine uses his Dictaphone.'

Recipe for perfect happiness:

1. A man with a 12-inch penis who can satisfy you all night.

2. A caring man who will do all the housework and wait on you hand and foot.

3. A rich man who showers you with presents.

4. Making sure men 1,2 and 3 never ever meet.

What's the difference between
A Midsummer Night's Dream
and *Much Ado About Nothing*?
**Nine inches is a midsummer
night's dream – three inches
is much ado about nothing.**

Two brothers are having a medical, and the doctor comments on the unusual length of their penises. 'Yes, sir, we got them from our mother.' 'Your mother? Surely you inherited them from your father?' **'No, sir. You see our mother only has one arm.'** 'One arm? What's that got to do with the length of your penises?' 'Well, she had to lift us out of the bath somehow.'

Better to have
loved and lost
a short man
**then never
to have loved
a tall one.**

What do you say to an
impotent man?
'No hard feelings.'

SHE'LL BE
COMING
ROUND THE
MOUNTAIN

When God had finished making Adam and Eve he told them he had two gifts left over. 'First, the gift of being able to pee standing up...' Before He'd even finished, Adam started shouting, 'Oh yes, pee standing up – I'll have that, that'd be brilliant! I'd love that! Please, please, please...'

So God, with an indulgent smile, gives Adam the ability to pee standing up. 'What's the other one?' asks Eve. 'Oh, multiple orgasms...'

Orgasm types

Sex with a rower: oargasm

Sex after falling out of bed: floorgasm

Wet dream: snoregasm

Group sex: fourgasm

Sex for hours and hours: soregasm

Cheap sex: poorgasm

Noisy sex: roargasm

Nymphomaniac sex: Iwantmoregasm

Sex on the beach: shoregasm

Swedish sex: smorgasborgasm

Competitive sex: scoregasm

Sex with a pig: boargasm

Sex on holiday: tourgasm

Sex on the farm: tractorgasm

Sex with a Viking: Thorgasm

What do snails shout during sex?

'Slower! Slower!'

Little Johnny's maths teacher asks him to define 'average'. 'It's a kind of bed, Miss,' says little Johnny. **'A bed?'** 'Yes, I overheard my mum saying she has three orgasms a week on an average.'

'Did you come on the bus, Grandma?'

'Yes, dear, but I passed it off as an asthma attack.'

A woman walks into the dentist's, takes off her knickers and sits in the chair with a leg over each arm. 'Madam, I think there's some mistake,' says the dentist, 'the gynaecologist's surgery is on the next floor.' 'No mistake,' replies the woman, 'yesterday you put in my husband's new dentures. Today I want you to take them out.'

Why do men prefer to marry virgins?

That way the wife won't know what she's missing.

Bob is having a drink with his friend Bill. 'Do you know,' says Bill, 'there are four kinds of female orgasm: positive, negative, religious and fake.' 'How do you tell them apart?' asks Bob. 'If it's positive, she shouts, "Oh yes, yes!", negative is when she shouts, "Oh no, no!" and "Oh God, oh God!" is the religious orgasm.' 'But what does she shout when it's fake?' asks Bob. 'She shouts "Bob! Bob!"'

Heard about the new stealth condom?

You won't see him coming.

A woman on her deathbed tells her husband to look in the big trunk under the bed. He opens it and finds three eggs and a thousand pounds in cash. 'Every time I faked an orgasm with you, I took an egg and I put it in the trunk,' **says the woman. 'Not bad,' thinks the man, 'three fakes in all these years of marriage.' So he asks the woman, 'But what about the thousand pounds?' 'Every time I got up to a dozen eggs, I sold them.'**

How many honest, intelligent, attractive, caring men does it take to truly satisfy a woman?
Both of them.

'You never shout my name when you come!'
'No, I don't want to wake you up.'

45% of women celebrate National Orgasm Day every year. The rest just pretend.

How can you tell when a blond guy has an orgasm?
He drops his kebab.

According to a recent survey, 85% of women masturbate in the shower and the other 15% sing. And do you know what they sing?
Thought not.

I was not faking it – I was just practising so I don't completely forget how to do it.

An ambulance is called one Sunday morning to a 99-year-old man who has died in bed. To their amazement, he appears to have died while making love to his 98-year-old wife. 'We've always done it on Sunday morning,' explains his tearful wife, 'because at our age, you have to take it slow. We'd listen to the church bells, ding-dong, ding-dong, in-out, in-out – and we'd still be doing it now, if that damned ice-cream van hadn't turned up.'

For their 50th wedding anniversary, Bill and Sue go back to the cottage where they spent their honeymoon. As they stroll along a country path, Bill says, 'Look, do you remember that tree by the fence?' 'I certainly do,' blushes Sue, 'that's where we had the hottest sex of our honeymoon.' Well, they're both still hot for each other, so they have a look around and, seeing there's nobody in sight, they're soon over by the tree, with Sue leaning against the fence, her skirt hitched up and Bill going at it like a man

50 years younger. In no time, Sue is yelling and thrashing about, and she doesn't stop until Bill is exhausted and has to sit down on the grass. 'I can't have lost my touch,' he says proudly, 'I don't remember you going that wild 50 years ago.' '50 years ago,' says Sue, 'that fence wasn't electric.'

KINKS
AND
QUIRKS

What's the difference between an ice cream and a masochist?

An ice cream is often licked but never beaten...

A newly-wed couple arrive at their honeymoon hotel, and ask for a double room. 'Since it's your honeymoon,' says the receptionist, 'wouldn't you like the bridal suite?' **'No, it's all right,' says the bridegroom, 'I'll just hold on to her ears till she gets the hang of it.'**

What's black and white and red-hot?

A nun with pierced nipples.

Why didn't the flasher take early retirement?

He decided he could stick it out for another year.

What's the difference between sexy and kinky?

Sexy is using a feather – kinky is when it's still attached to the chicken.

How many perverts does it take to put in a light bulb?

Only one, but you have to go to Accident and Emergency to get it taken out.

Why is rimming like drinking Snakebite?

They both leave you shit-faced.

What do you call a man who's gagged and tied to the bed?

Trustworthy.

How do you spot really sexy shoes?

You can get them off with one finger.

What's the difference between a masochist and a mosquito?
If you hit a mosquito, it'll stop eating you.

What kind of sweets do perverts eat?
S&M&Ms

What does a transvestite do at Christmas?
Eat, drink and be Mary.

Why is virgin wool so expensive?
Because you can only get it from ugly sheep.

What's the word for a man who's watching a woman undress?

Grateful.

A van driver is driving along when he sees a woman dressed in a PVC suit hitch-hiking. He stops to give her a lift and after a couple of miles she asks if he wants sex. They're going at it in the back, and she starts shouting, 'Spank me, spank me!' So he spanks her and she gets more and more excited. Then she starts shouting, 'Whip me, whip me!' 'I haven't got a whip,' he protests. 'Well, there must be something you can use – why not pull the radio aerial off and use that?' So he pulls the aerial off the van and whips her with that. Afterwards she's really sore, so she goes to the doctor and shows him the marks on her bottom from the whipping. 'Did you get these marks having sex?' asks the doctor. 'Yes, I did,' she says. 'I thought so. This is the worst case of van-aerial disease I've ever seen.'

Why do sadists take so long to get to the point?

Because they're always beating around the bush.

An Englishman, an Irishman and a Scotsman are being interviewed for the priesthood and they're told they have to pass a celibacy test to see if they're capable of controlling their carnal urges. They stand naked in a room and a small bell is tied to each of their pricks to reveal the slightest arousal. A beautiful woman is then brought in and she starts to perform a striptease. **'Ting-a-ling!'** the Irishman's bell rings as his prick stirs uncontrollably. Then the naked woman approaches the Scotsman and starts to blow on his neck. **'Ting-a-ling!'** the Scotsman's bell rings. Now the two have huge erections, but the Englishman is not aroused at all. The woman runs her hands all over his naked body, but nothing – his bell remains silent. At last the priest says, 'Enough! You have proved yourself worthy of the priesthood. As for you other two, your punishment shall be a severe caning.' **'Ting-a-ling!'** goes the Englishman's bell.

A woman stopped to admire her neighbour's tomatoes. 'How do you get them so red?' she asks. 'I must admit,' he says, 'I'm a bit of an exhibitionist and I like to flash in my garden. I think the tomatoes blush every time I do it, that's why they're so red.' 'Thank you, I might try that myself,' she says. A few weeks later the same man sees the woman digging her own garden, but her tomatoes are still green. 'So you didn't try my technique?' he asks her. 'Oh yes,' she says. 'My tomatoes stayed the same – but my cucumbers are huge.'

What's the difference between a pickpocket and a voyeur?

A pickpocket snatches your watch and a voyeur watches your snatch.

What do you call a thick book about voyeurism?

A peeping tome.

Hear about the transvestite who lost the high-heel-wearing contest?
He suffered the agony of defeat.

Ever thought of dating a necrophiliac?
Over my dead body!

What's the difference between a man and a vibrator?
They haven't made a vibrator that can mow the lawn.

An old rancher marries a young wife, hoping she can help with the hard work, but soon it's clear that they need more help, so they hire a strapping young cowboy to help around the place. After a month the rancher's wife says to the rancher, 'Hank's worked so hard, I think he deserves a night off. Let's tell him he can ride into town, and I'll wait up to let him in when he gets back.' The rancher agrees, and Hank rides into town.

When he gets back, the rancher's wife is sitting in the kitchen waiting for him. 'Come in, Hank,' she says, 'now, I want you to take off my shoes.' 'Yes, Ma'am,' says Hank, and he takes off her little button boots. 'Very good, Hank. **Now take off my skirt**.' So Hank slips off her skirt. 'Now Hank, take off my stockings and my corset.' So Hank takes off her stockings and her corset. 'And finally, Hank, I want you to **take off my panties**.' So Hank takes off her panties. **'Very good, Hank. Now, if I ever catch you wearing my clothes to town again, you're fired.'**

A man walks into the bedroom naked but entirely wrapped in clingfilm and says to his wife, 'Tell me the truth, do you think I'm a pervert?' 'I don't know about pervert,' replies his wife, 'but I can clearly see you're nuts.'

A nun gets into a taxi. As he drives her along, the taxi driver says he has a confession to make – he's always had a sexual thing about nuns. As he's just been told he has a terminal illness it would mean a lot to him if he could have sex with a nun just once before he dies. 'Well, my son,' says the nun, 'in view of your tragic circumstances, it is my duty to do what I can for you. I will have sex with you on one condition – obviously I can't get pregnant, so I'll have to take it up the tradesman's entrance.' The taxi driver gets in the back, lifts up the nun's habit and buggers her soundly.

Afterwards, the taxi driver starts to cry. 'I feel so guilty,' he says. 'I lied to you to get you to have sex with me. I don't really have a terminal illness at all.' 'That's all right,' says the nun, 'I lied to you as well – my name's Kevin and I'm on my way to a fancy dress party.'

A punk rocker gets on a bus: he's pierced and tattooed, with multicoloured hair in a big mohican. He sees an old man staring and says 'What's the matter old boy – didn't you ever do anything wild in your life?' 'Yes,' says the old man. 'I had sex with a parrot once, and I was just wondering if you were my son.'

Why couldn't they get funding for a porn film about flagellation, bestiality and necrophilia? **Everyone said they were flogging a dead horse.**

What's a shepherd's favourite love song?
'I only have eyes for ewe!'

Some people like bondage, but it's knot for everyone.

Perverts Dictionary

Biodegradable: likes to be humiliated by lovers of either sex

Combination: to ahieve orgasm in order of nationality

Deferred: shaved pubic hair

Erectile: to be turned on by flooring

Gaggle: sound made by someone trying to laugh while wearing a gag

Hamstring: what Hollywood stars do with a small rodent

Hermitage: when the woman wears gloves

Hertz: sadistic sex

Liposuction: a blowjob

Megahertz: really sadistic sex

Multitude: oral sex with lots of partners

Mystical: a dominatrix with a feather duster

Negligent: a man who likes to wear frilly nightwear

Permitted: wearing gloves while dressed as Catwoman

Rectitude: rimming

Referred: pubic hair grown back

Stalemate: wife-swapping

Tourist liaison: a pair of handcuffs

Why did the sadist steal the batteries for the vibrator? **Because he liked to take charge.**

Why did the pervert fancy the chicken? **He thought it was poultry in motion.**

My husband bought a waterbed but then we started to drift apart.

A woman passes a pet shop and sees a sign, 'Clitoris-licking Frog', so she goes in and says, 'I've come about the clitoris-licking frog,' and the assistant answers, 'Oui, Madame?'

Why does a man with a pierced willy make the best husband?

He's experienced pain and he knows how to buy jewellery.

I wanted to be a streaker but I wasn't suited for it.

A man goes to a brothel and asks for the kinkiest girl they have. 'I'm sorry, sir, all our girls are busy, but if you like you can have the pig.' He thinks it's pretty kinky, so he has sex with the pig. Next week he's back, asking for the kinkiest girl they have. 'I'm sorry, sir, all our girls are busy.' 'Well, can I have the pig again?' 'No, sorry, sir, no pig, but if you like you can go into the room at the end and watch.' **So he goes into the room at the end and there are a dozen guys all masturbating, watching through a pane of glass while a woman licks melted chocolate off a man who is tied to the bed.** 'Wow!' he says, 'That's pretty hot!' 'You think this is good,' says one of the other guys, 'there was some pervert in there last week, having sex with a pig.'

It's okay to use food in sex, but be safe – always use a condiment.

Some perverts like to watch a woman wrestle, but most men prefer to see her box.

What do you get if you cross a pervert and a hamster?

Letters from animal rights campaigners.

How do you know when you're at a sadist's wedding?

They use real pain for the toasts instead of champagne.

A woman goes into a sex shop and asks to see the dildos. The assistant shows her a black one, but she says it's too small. He shows her a pink one, but that's still too small. Then he shows her a chrome one, but she says none of them will do. Finally, she points to the big tartan one on the top shelf, and says she'll have that one. A few minutes later the manager gets back from lunch and asks how it's going. 'Great – I sold one black dildo, two pink dildos, three chrome dildos – and your Thermos flask.'